THE JOURNEY CONTINUES
VOL 10

FAITH HOPE LOVE

WILLIAM HATFIELD

ISBN: 978-1-9992526-0-1

DEDICATION

I DEDICATE THIS BOOK TO THE THIRSTY AND HUNGRY SAINTS OF GOD THAT DESIRE AN INTIMACY WITH THE HOLY SPIRIT LIKE NO OTHER. MY PRAYER IS THAT YOU CAN FIND THIS JOURNEY AS A SOURCE OF ENCOURAGEMENT, STRENGTH AND POWER TO OVERCOME LIFE'S STRUGGLES AND WALK IN A GREATER SENSE OF FREEDOM AND RELATIONSHIP WITH THE HOLY SPIRIT AND ALL WITHIN YOUR SPHERE OF INFLUENCE.

ACKNOWLEDGEMENTS

We are all on a journey through life! I want to thank all my family and friends who stand besides me and encourage me when times are tough.

I especially want to thank my aunt Viola for all her work in editing and preparing the manuscript of my first book for publishing. The knowledge she shared will help me to continue writing. Her confidence in me ignited a gift I never realized I had. God created me with many gifts and one of them is to be a writer. Thank you Jesus for your great love.

PROLOGUE

How Faith, Hope and Love Work Together
To Give You Confidence in God

Sometimes these three attributes are a
mystery to us so in this writing I am
attempting to demystify them.

**And now these three remain: faith, hope
and love. But the greatest of these is love.**
1 Corinthians 13:13 |

CONTENTS

1 HOPE

WHAT IS HOPE AND WHY DO WE NEED IT? I guess the first thing is to look at the definition of hope.

hope

[hōp]

NOUN

hopes *(plural noun)*

1. a feeling of expectation and desire for a certain thing to happen.
   "he looked through her belongings in the hope of coming across some information" · "I had high hopes of making the Olympic team"
   synonyms:
   aspiration · desire · wish · expectation · ambition · aim · plan · dream · daydream · pipe dream · longing · yearning · craving · hankering
   - a person or thing that may help or save someone.

"their only hope is surgery"
synonyms:
<u>optimism</u> · grounds for hope · <u>promise</u> · <u>light at the end of the tunnel</u>
antonyms:
<u>Pessimism</u>

- Grounds for believing that something good may happen.
  "He does see some hope for the future"
  Synonyms:
  <u>hopefulness</u> · <u>optimism</u> · <u>expectation</u> · <u>expectancy</u> · <u>confidence</u> · <u>faith</u> · <u>trust</u> · <u>belief</u> · <u>conviction</u> · <u>assurance</u>

2. *archaic*
   A feeling of trust.
   "Our private friendship, upon hope and affiance whereof, I presume to be your petitioner"

VERB

Hopes *(third person present)* · **hoped** *(past tense)* · **hoped** *(past participle)* · **hoping** *(present participle)*

3. Want something to happen or be the case.

"He's hoping for an offer of compensation" · "I hope that the kids are OK"

synonyms:

<u>expect</u> · <u>anticipate</u> · look for · wait for · be hopeful of · <u>pin one's hopes on</u> · <u>want</u> · wish for · dream of · hope against hope for

antonyms:

despair of

- intend if possible to do something. "we're hoping to address all these issues"

  synonyms:

  <u>aim</u> · <u>intend</u> · be looking · have the/every intention · have in mind · <u>plan</u> · <u>aspire</u>

From these definitions it seems hope is very important to the human equation. From the first definition we see wish, daydream and pipe dream. These three suggest fantasies of the flesh such as abundance of money and things so a person can do whatever they want when they want.

In my thinking hope is a condition of the soul. When everything in the natural is going our way we feel fulfilled so we can wish for our pipe dreams and daydream about stuff. What if everything is not going our way? Trials, tribulations and persecutions seem rampant in our lives. When I look around I see only brokenness. I look into my life there's brokenness. I look at others and I find broken hearts everywhere. At the end of the year when I sit down and thinking about my own life as well as the lives of others which made me very disturbed.

Why there's so much brokenness?

I know there's an answer to that question … But all of us we don't stop living… We keep doing our part of the responsibilities, fulfilling whatever is required of us, making our bosses, pastors and government officials happy, and satisfying our family members and so on…

But most of the times we drag our lives… like I do sometimes. I live on a life of pretension. Now pretentious life never allows us to live freely or in liberty. So we can't term that living as "live in hope".

The Greek word for hope is *hopemeno* which means "to wait," "to be patient," "to endure" till something happens. And till something happens how should we behave, what should be our reactions, how we should stay?

The modern idea of hope is "to wish for, to expect, but without certainty of the fulfillment; to desire very much, but with no real assurance of getting your desire." According to the biblical usage, hope is an indication of certainty. "Hope" in Scripture means "a strong and confident expectation."

Yes, if we are hopeful we should be happy, energetic, positive, enthusiastic, jovial, and cheerful and so on… because our confidence on something or someone for which we are hopeful of something good to happen is of utmost value and on truth. Hope is not always about something good will happen to us only but it might be something good will happen around us... And our suffering will be credited to that good which will happen around us.

Hope I am making it myself clear by what I said above...

2 LIVING IN HOPE

To live in hope is to first change our focus. In the definition I noticed number 2: *archaic*

A feeling of trust.
"Our private friendship, upon hope and affiance whereof, I presume to be your petitioner"
ar·cha·ic
/ärˈkāik/

adjective
adjective: **archaic**

1. very old or old-fashioned.

"prisons are run on archaic methods"

synonyms: obsolete, obsolescent, out of date, anachronistic, old-fashioned, outmoded, behind the times, bygone, antiquated, antique, superannuated,

antediluvian, past its prime,
having seen better days,
olde worlde, oldfangled;

To me the archaic definition is where I want to go. A private friendship with someone who is reliable, trustworthy and loves me unconditionally. Someone who has my best interests in mind and wants to see me fulfill my destiny.

For I know the plans I have for you, declares the Lord, plans to prosper you and not to harm you, plans to give you hope and a future.

Jeremiah 29:11 | <u>NIV</u>

When I focus on my physical condition and circumstances, my hope is filled with despair, wishing something good will happens rather than being confident that things will change for the better. I should look to David for an example when he was going through tough situations.

Why, my soul, are you downcast? Why so disturbed within me? Put your hope in God, for I will yet praise him, my Savior and my God.

Psalm 42:11 | NIV

He knew how to change his focus:

But those who hope in the Lord will renew their strength. They will soar on wings like eagles; they will run and not grow weary, they will walk and not be faint.

Isaiah 40:31 | NIV

My focus should be on God's word and not my circumstances.

May the God of hope fill you with all joy and peace as you trust in him, so that you may overflow with hope by the power of the Holy Spirit.

Romans 15:13 | NIV

My relationship with Jesus through the Holy Spirit and God's word will produce a hope in me that will be AN ACTUAL BLUEPRINT FOR FAITH TO WORK.

Now faith is confidence in what we hope for and assurance about what we do not see.

Hebrews 11:1 | NIV
And now these three remain: faith, hope and love. But the greatest of these is love.
1 Corinthians 13:13 | NIV

As I study God's word the bible and continually fellowship with the Holy Spirit my hope and confidence grows. When I don't despair and fear take its place in my soul.

3 FAITH

How Faith And Hope Work Together To Give You Confidence in God

Faith and hope are vitally connected and it's important to understand the value they have together so we can have an unshakeable confidence in God.

To be honest, both faith and hope have always been a bit of a mystery for me. By nature, they both seem a bit vague. You cannot touch them, hear them or see them yet you see the evidence of each: people saved, prayers answered and a joyful outlook of the future, to name a few.

One thing we do know, there is a vital connection between faith and hope. One cannot live without the other.

It says in Hebrews 11:1 "Now faith is the assurance of things hoped for, the conviction of things not seen."

1. Faith is given by God to know God. Faith's object is God (His goodness and power). Faith grows through revelation of who He is by the Holy Spirit. It gains strength as we know God better.

2. Faith's anchor is assessing accurately WHO God is.
This is vital. When we understand God rightly then we can confidently say, "all things are possible with God." When we rightly understand who God is and continue to grow in this understanding then our faith increases. On the other hand, when we misunderstand who God is, faith wanes and hope is not even in view. This is huge!

3. Faith is active.

Faith lives and accesses God's Kingdom. Faith has movement. Faith is best defined by demonstration.

4. Faith is the substance of hope and hope awakens faith.

There is an interactive dynamic between faith and hope. Faith gives life to hope and hope strengthens our faith. You can't have one without the other.

5. Faith is coming into agreement with what God is saying and hope anticipates its reality.
Every promise, every prophetic word God has given carries with it life that can only be activated by faith. Faith comes into agreement and believes each promise, prophetic word and/or written Word.

6. The proof of our faith is hope.
When we have hope in God we prove that faith is active.

7. Without faith, hope is only a wish (powerless). But when we have hope in God, faith is powerful.
A wish is hope without God. It's something we long for but it's generally not connected to God. Biblical hope has as its foundation faith in God.

8. Unbelief honors what we see as impossible. Faith honors what we believe is possible.
Unbelief is simply faith in the inferior.

9. Hope looks to the future while faith lays hold of the present.

10. By faith we understand (Hebrews 11:3) Most of us need to understand something first before we have faith but that's not what the Bible says. The Bible says that we have faith in order to understand. Faith is understanding.

11. Faith is not presumption.

The difference between faith and presumption is faith is our response to God's word of revelation; presumption is our expectation of God to do something He did not say.

Regardless of what we are going through we can put our faith in God and find hope. When we rightly discover God we will undoubtedly find faith and be filled with hope. When both of these are active, we will truly have an unshakable confidence in God to meet every situation we face.

Faith also works by love: Galatians 5:6 "For in Christ Jesus, neither circumcision nor uncircumcision counts for anything, but *only faith working through love*." Here it is clear that faith is conjoined with love—that the two virtues together are essential to life in Christ.

4 LOVE

There are many kinds of love. Let's look at them.

The 7 Types of Love You'll Probably Experience in This Life

Discover all the different types of love in the world, from ancient Greek terms for love to modern types of love.

7 Types of Love, according to the ancient Greeks

The ancient Greeks had seven words for love that corresponded to different types of love, ranging from physical love (eros) to purely spiritual love (agape). Here are the seven kinds of love according to the ancient Greeks.

1. Eros: Love of the body

Eros was the Greek God of love and sexual desire. He was shooting golden arrows into the hearts of both mortals and immortals without warning. The Greeks feared that kind of love the most because it was dangerous and could get them into the most trouble. Eros is defined as divine beauty or lust. Eros is mainly based on sexual attraction and it is where the term "erotica" came from.

<u>Example of Eros love:</u> A young couple that meets and immediately feels attracted, and lustful, towards one another.

2. Philia: <u>Love of the mind</u>

Also known as brotherly love, *Philia* represents the sincere and platonic love. The kind of love you have for your brother or a really good friend. It was more valuable and more cherished than Eros. Philia exists when people share the same values and dispositions with someone and the feelings are reciprocated.

<u>Example of Philia love:</u> Two friends talk

about how deeply they understand each other, and how that security and openness causes them to feel comfortable and taken care of.

3. Ludus: Playful love

Ludus is the flirtatious and teasing kind of love, the love mostly accompanied by dancing or laughter. It's the child-like and fun kind of love. If you think about it; this generation loves Ludus more than anything else.

Example of Ludus love: Modern love at its finest, Ludus love is best described by thinking of two people who just want to have fun together, with little need for security or roots.

4. Pragma: Longstanding love

The everlasting love between married couples which develops over a long period of time. *Pragma* was the highest form of love; the true commitment that comes from understanding, compromise and tolerance. It is pragmatic this is why it is referred to as "standing in love" rather than "falling in love" because it grows over time and requires profound understanding between lovers who have been together for many years.

Example of Pragma love: Think about your grandparents, and how they have endured so much, but have always chosen each other.

5. Agape: Love of the soul

Agape love is selfless love, the love for humanity. It is the closest to unconditional love. The love you give without expecting anything in return reflected in all charitable acts. It is the compassionate love that makes us sympathize with, help and connect to people we don't know. The world needs more Agape love.

Example of Agape love: The person in your

life that is always giving to others, and needing nothing in return. This is the way they show their love, and this is the way they are energized through love. By giving all that they have, and all that they are, to those around them, they find beauty in life.

6. Philautia: Love of the self

The ancient Greeks divided *Philautia* into two kinds: There is one that is pure selfish and seeks pleasure, fame, and wealth often leading to narcissism and there is another healthy kind of love we give ourselves. Philautia is essential for any relationship, we can only love others if we truly love ourselves and we can only care for others if we truly care for ourselves.

Example of Philautia love: Selfish Philautia love is the kind of love that takes and does not give back in return — this is someone who only uses others to excel in life. Think about the social climbers of the world. On the other hand, the positive kind of

Philautia can be seen in a couple that is a union, not a melting pot. They both do their own things, but they come together and support each other's own growth.

7. Storge: Love of the child

Storge is the love parents naturally feel for their children. It's based on natural feelings and effortless love. Storge is the love that knows forgiveness, acceptance and sacrifice. It is the one that makes you feel secure, comfortable and safe.

<u>Example of Storge love:</u> Think about the kind of love your mother gives you, or your very best friend. It is rooted in friendship, and understanding, but there is also a deep emotional connection there.

In today's world most human love is bankrupt. This is evident in divorce, school shootings and violence rising amongst the populace. I have worked with friends who ran an orphanage and watched parents abandon their children because the children were an inconvenience. The kind of love I want to look at is agape or God's love.

Agape (Ancient Greek ἀγάπη, *agapē*) is a Greco-Christian term referring to love, "the highest form of love, charity" and "the love of God for man and of man for God". The word is not to be confused with philia, brotherly love, or <u>philautia</u>, self-love, as it embraces a universal, unconditional love that transcends and persists regardless of circumstance. It goes beyond just the emotions to the extent of seeking the best for others. The noun form first occurs in the Septuagint, but the verb form goes as far back as Homer, translated literally as affection, as in "greet with affection" and "show affection for the dead". Other ancient authors have used forms of the word to denote love of a spouse or family, or affection for a particular activity, in contrast to eros (an affection of a sexual nature).

Within Christianity, *agape* is considered to be the love originating from God or Christ for humankind. In the New Testament, it refers to the covenant love of God for humans, as well as the human reciprocal love for God; the term necessarily extends to the love of one's fellow man.

For God so loved the world, that he gave his only begotten Son, that whosoever believeth in him should not perish, but have everlasting life.

— *John 3:16, KJV*

There is a place we have to come to in our Christian walk to be flowing in, in order for faith and hope to be grounded and rooted. Grounded in the word of God and rooted in agape love.

1 John 4:8 King James Version (KJV)

[8] He that loveth not knoweth not God; for God is love.

1 John 4:16 King James Version (KJV)
16 And we have known and believed the love that God hath to us. God is love; and he that dwelleth in love dwelleth in God and God in him.

How do we dwell or live in love? When we do then we live in God and god lives in us. To live is so different from existing. To live means to be active in fellowship, adventures I both the natural realm and spiritual realm. After all God is a spirit and we are a spirit who owns a SOUL AND LIVES IN A BODY.

We need to see what the bible says; **1 Corinthians 13**

1

If I speak in the tongues of men and of angels, but have not love, I am only a resounding gong or a clanging cymbal.

2

If I have the gift of prophecy and can fathom all mysteries and all knowledge, and if I have a faith that can move mountains, but have not love, I am nothing.

3

If I give all I possess to the poor and surrender my body to the flames, but have not love, I gain nothing.

4

Love is patient, love is kind. It does not envy, it does not boast, it is not proud.

5

It is not rude, it is not self-seeking, it is not easily angered, it keeps no record of wrongs.

6

Love does not delight in evil but rejoices with the truth.

7

It always protects, always trusts, always hopes, always perseveres.

8

Love never fails. But where there are prophecies, they will cease; where there are tongues, they will be stilled; where there is knowledge, it will pass away.

9

For we know in part and we prophesy in part,

10

but when perfection comes, the imperfect disappears.

11

When I was a child, I talked like a child; I thought like a child, I reasoned like a child. When I became a man, I put childish ways behind me.

12

Now we see but a poor reflection as in a mirror; then we shall see face to face. Now I know in part; then I shall know fully, even as I am fully known.

13

And now these three remain: faith, hope and love. But the greatest of these is love.

People automatically default to human love when confronted and human love being bankrupt leads to anger, offence and bitterness when confronted.

I would like to share a vision I had while I attended victory harvest fellowship in Camrose Alberta. During praise and worship I had the following vision; I saw people walking through a path in the wilderness not as a group on one path but individuals on their own paths. On each path there were obstacles to try and slow them down from reaching a destination. Couples didn't share a path nor families. Each individual walked their own path. Eventually we all came out of the wilderness into a plush meadow. We greeted each other and looked forward across the meadow where we could see Jesus standing. We heard him say "hear me talk continue to walk." We continued through the meadow until we came to the edge of a cliff. Standing at the edge of the cliff we looked over and down and about ten thousand feet we noticed a river flowing through the bottom. We looked straight forward at Jesus who was floating in the air. Jesus said "the next step will take you into my dimension and you will be free from all your works." The vision ended and I shared it with the congregation and a lady said that she wanted to hear the sermon on that vision.

I believe what the Holy Spirit is trying to tell us when we choose to walk in agape or God's love we will experience freedom from our own efforts of trying to please people and God. I believe to walk in agape love we must develop the fruit of the spirit in our lives. Galatians 5:22-23 New King James Version (NKJV)
[22] But the fruit of the Spirit is love, joy, peace, longsuffering, kindness, goodness, faithfulness, [23] gentlene ss, self-control. Against such there is no law.

Use your words to develop the fruit of the spirit and agape love in your life and watch faith and hope be rooted in love and work at greater levels in your life.

EPILOGUE.

THIS IS MY JOURNEY TO TRY AND UNDERSTAND THE SCRIPTURE **And now these three remain: faith, hope and love. But the greatest of these is love.** I HOPE I HAVE SHED SOME LIGHT ON YOUR UNDERSTANDING AND YOUR DESIRE TO FELLOWSHIP WITH THE Holy SPIRIT INTENSIFIES.

ABOUT THE AUTHOR

BIO

William carries the anointing of a prophet and psalmist. He is also a Bible teacher, author and international speaker. He operates in all of the Spiritual gifts. He uses the gifts as the Holy Spirit wills. One of William's great desires is to lead others to Christ and to follow Holy Spirit wherever He leads.

YOU CAN VISIT MY WEBSITE
WWW.PSALMISTWILLIAM.CA
FOR ENCOURAGING PSALMS AND TO BUY OTHER BOOKS I HAVE WRITTEN